HELL'S ANGELS BIKER WARS
The Rock Machine Massacre

Volume VIII

by **RJ Parker**

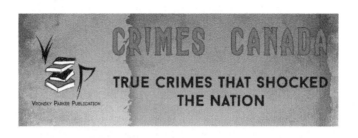

HELL'S ANGELS BIKER WARS
The Rock Machine Massacre

Volume VIII

by RJ Parker

Crimes Canada
True Crimes That Shocked The Nation
www.CrimesCanada.com

ISBN-13: 978-1517198718
ISBN-10: 1517198712

Published in Canada

Copyrights

Kindle Unlimited

Enjoy these top rated true crime eBooks from VP Publications **FREE** as part of your Kindle Unlimited subscription. You can read it on your Kindle Fire, on a computer via Kindle Cloud Reader or on any smartphone with the free Kindle reading app.

View All True Crime and Crime Fiction Books by RJ Parker Publishing at the following Amazon Links:

Amazon Kindle - USA
Amazon Kindle - Canada
Amazon Kindle - UK
Amazon Kindle - Australia

TABLE OF CONTENTS

An Introduction to Biker Culture

In the twentieth century, a unique social phenomenon was noted to appear. This social phenomenon was the creation of sub cultures. Starting with the hippie movement of the sixties to Gothic subculture in the present day, society has segmented itself into niches which are occupied by people who are interested in what the message of the subculture is. The hippies were all about peace and freedom, Goths are generally all about doom and misery. It is a testament to the popularization of individuality over social integration in the latter half of the twentieth century that society formed within itself so many pockets for people to settle into and feel like they belong.

Not all of the subcultures that developed during the twentieth century were positive for society as a whole. Subcultures, by their very definition, are celebrations of individual traits and preferences, and as most people very well know, there are a lot of human traits that are not exactly worthy of celebration. Hence, many of these subcultures became embroiled in illegal activities, with violence and decadence becoming intrinsic parts of the lifestyles of the members of these subcultures.

An example of such subcultures that had negative connotations associated with them is the biker subculture. ([1]) Although it would be unfair to state that all adherents to the biker way of life are criminals, during the last two decades of the twentieth century, members of biker gangs caused some of the most violent incidents in the history of North America. Although they have not been romanticized the way the Italian mafia has, nor have they been depicted as often as Latin gangs, the Irish mob or the Russian mafia, biker gangs have always been a major part of organized crime across the world.

Biker culture can trace its history to the very beginning of the twentieth century with the creation of the New York Motorcycle Club in 1903. The popularity of the motorcycle was what led to the creation of this motorcycle club, a popularity that was the result of the individuality and power that motorcycles tended to represent. Motorcycle clubs were initially little more than havens for motorcycle enthusiasts, with the bulk of the membership being people who simply admired motorcycles for the freedom that they provided.

The motorcycle is not a family vehicle. It is, in fact, possibly the only motorized vehicle that signifies individuality and a lone wolf mentality above all else. Therefore, it was only natural for the motorcycle to begin attracting some less than savory characters, which meant that these motorcycles clubs started to become havens for people who felt like they could not belong anywhere else. The tendency of such clubs to attract people that exhibited antisocial behavior played a big role in the development of outlaw biker culture over the course of the twentieth century. So many antisocial people congregating in the same place only exacerbated the state of mind that these people were in.

The Post War Ideological Revolution

The true essence of the outlaw biker gang came about after the Second World War. (^{2}) This was a time of mass social reform, with the terrible losses that were incurred during the war resulting in a massive paradigm shift that ended up altering the ideological status quo. The war gave birth to many cultural movements, as the people that ended up inspiring the genesis of subculture, people such as the Beatles, all grew up being affected by this war, and thus their own ideologies were shaped by the austerity of post-war life.

The same austerity of post-war life was probably one of the two most important factors that resulted in the development of biker subculture. The post-war climate was stifling to say the least, at least as far as finances were concerned. This was an inevitable result of the immense financial toll that the war took on the countries that participated in it. It was this stifling financial climate that caused so many people to seek a lifestyle of rebellion, a lifestyle where rules did not exist and people could do what they wanted when they wanted it. The other important factor that went into the creation of biker subculture actually went in direct opposition of the previous factor. The general aura of sobriety and austerity that followed the Second World War was opposed by the flower power-influenced musical revolution that took place in the sixties. Even the era directly following the war, the fifties to be specific, saw a rise in a more sexual version of music spearheaded by Elvis. Music was starting to become about freedom, it was starting to become a way for people to experience catharsis. It was, in essence, becoming about freedom.

As far as music is concerned, there is one song in particular that has influenced biker subculture over all others and, in fact, exemplifies practically everything that the biker subculture stands for. The song is called "*Born to be Wild*" by the band Steppenwolf (Lyrics) ([3]). This song is essentially about how one is naturally programmed for a life of freedom, and romanticizes the open highway as the ultimate source of said freedom. Biker subculture took a lot of inspiration from this song, and a lot of stylistic cues that bikers followed were taken from the clothing style of the members of Steppenwolf.

Bikers to Outlaws

The gradual rise in the popularity of biker gangs led to a solidification of most of the major aspects of the subculture, such as the attire they wear along with the activities that they participate in. But, starting in the 1970s, the biker subculture began to take on a more sinister demeanor, particularly with regards to the activities that certain biker gangs would get involved in. With so many antisocial individuals attracted to the concept of freedom that the motorcycle afforded to them coming together, it was only a matter of time before the combined aggression of these bikers would result in negative consequences.

As biker subculture developed, many biker gangs began to give into mob mentality and thus began to get involved in illegal activities. The biker subculture places particular importance on machismo and aggression, something that was heavily influenced by the type of people that tended to be attracted to the biker way of life. With so much machismo and aggression coming together, along with the mob mentality that comes with groups that are so large, the incorporation of illicit activities into the overall ideology of biker subculture was inevitable.

The major illegal activity that bikers became involved in had to do with illegal substances, particularly drugs. Biker gangs have been popular middle men in the drug trade, providing a means of transporting drugs from the source where the drugs are actually created to the low level criminals who would actually sell the drugs. Hence, bikers are not exactly drug dealers. Rather, they have always aspired to be the people that the drug dealers would purchase their products from.

The drug that biker gangs are most commonly associated with is Crystal meth, short for crystal methamphetamine, ([4]) although some biker gangs have been known to deal in heroin and cocaine as well. But Crystal meth holds a distinct place in biker subculture because it is the only drug that biker gangs have been known to manufacture themselves. The Crystal meth that biker gangs tend to manufacture is usually different from standard meth, as it often has a yellow or bluish hue to it and is referred to specifically as biker meth.

The aggression of biker gangs has allowed them to gain control of large parts of the drug trade in many cities, becoming major rivals for many criminal organizations. Such rivalries, notably fierce because of the value of what was being fought over, namely the drug trade, resulted in major catastrophes and occasionally outright war. One of the most severe wars in which biker gangs were involved was the Quebec Biker War, which involved two of the most prominent biker gangs in North America, namely the Hell's Angels and Bandidos.

The Quebec Biker War ([5]) is a good example of just how much damage biker gangs can cause if they are not controlled by law enforcement. It also provides us with an important case study which can be examined in order to ascertain just how seriously biker gangs should be taken.

It would be unfair to bikers in general to just assume that all bikers are involved in such illegal activities. Indeed, the majority of bikers are actually law-abiding citizens who just happen to have an affinity for motorcycles. According to the American Motorcyclist Association, 99% of all bikers are law-abiding citizens. But the illegal activities of the one-percent of bikers that are actually part of outlaw biker gangs tend to get more media coverage than the good that bikers do all over the world.

Outlaw biker gangs often intentionally distance themselves from the American Motorcyclist Association, as these outlaws share a mutual dislike of the organization. They do not follow the set of rules that members of the American Motorcyclist Association tend to follow, instead abiding by their own individual set of rules. The most important way in which some bikers distance themselves from the American Motorcyclist Association is by calling themselves 1%ers ([6]). This refers to the AMA's comment that only one percent of bikers are outlaws or criminals. Members of outlaw biker gangs tend to revel in this small rebellion against the system, and are usually proud of their status as criminals and outlaws as they believe that this status is an important part of the freedom that they so greatly desire.

Features and Traits of Outlaw Bikers

There are several ways in which a member of an outlaw biker gang can be recognized, as these bikers tend to flaunt their membership and way of life. The most commonly recognized visual identification of bikers, attire which has become an iconic and widely accepted part of the biker subculture, is the biker vest. This vest is often adorned with a variety of patches which allow members of gangs to identify their fellow gang members and to declare fealty to a particular gang.

These patches often have names of the biker gang that the individual is a part of, a recognizable biker term such as "1%er" or any other kind of symbol or phrase that would identify that person as a part of a biker gang. The wearing of a patch is more of a privilege than a right, one that is specifically reserved for fully inducted members of the biker gang in question. Members of outlaw biker gangs often get violent if they see a non member wearing biker-inspired clothing with a patch that is reserved for use by members of his gang.

Apart from leather vests adorned with patches, bikers are also known to possess long beards and frequently wear sunglasses. These features and accouterments are rarely the result of any practical requirement of being a member of an outlaw motorcycle gang. Such things are preferences of the bikers themselves and the image that the bikers are attempting to portray, one of rugged masculinity and fearlessness.

This fearlessness is actually an important part of biker philosophy. The motto of the vast majority of outlaw bikers is "*Respect few, fear none*". This motto fits the machismo that is so inherent in every aspect of the biker subculture. Strict adherence to this motto is also part of the reason why bikers have become such widely feared figures in the world of organized crime.

Out of all of the attributes that distinguish outlaw bikers, the most widely recognizable is, of course, the motorcycle. The choice of motorcycle often reflects the biker gang's political mentality, with more nationalist outfits purchasing solely nationally produced motorcycles as is the case with Hell's Angels and the motorcycle company Harley-Davidson. In all things, members of outlaw biker gangs attempt to display their individuality by flaunting their membership.

One aspect of biker gangs that sets them apart from most other organized crime syndicates is that they often have chapters or branches in several different countries. Indeed, Hell's Angels have chapters in four different continents, with each charter possessing a large chunk of the drug trade in its respective city. No other crime organization is as widespread as the most powerful biker gangs.

Biker Orientation

In the previous section, the fearlessness that permeates biker mentality is discussed. This bravery is an important part of the biker ideology, ([7]) which places great emphasis on machismo and superiority over others. Biker ideology plays an important role in their activities and provides an interesting insight into how bikers conduct their business.

For example, it is highly unusual for there to be a female member of an outlaw biker gang. Such a thing is to be expected, especially considering the fact that biker gangs place so much emphasis on masculinity. Indeed, women are treated more like objects than anything else. They are frequently abused at parties that biker gangs throw, and most members of outlaw biker gangs see women as little more than sex objects that they can use for pleasure. If they are not viewed as sex objects, they are certainly not seen to be equal to males.

The superiority of males over females is an important aspect of biker ideology, even though it doesn't really play a role in any of their activities. It is important because it exemplifies the biker belief that they are better than everyone else, superior in some way to all other people.

This superiority complex is also seen in the fact that biker gangs are, for the most part, racially homogeneous. Indeed, it is highly uncommon to see a biker that is anything other than white. This is partially why the traditional and stereotypical image of a biker is that of a white man with a long beard. Although it is not necessary that biker gangs follow an ideology of racial superiority or that they are racist, it is a trait that is commonly incorporated into outlaw biker gangs. Thus, it is not uncommon for biker gangs to be white supremacists or to believe, at least partially, in Nazi belief. There have been many instances of neo-Nazi groups ([8]) and biker gangs collaborating or even sharing members, and there have also been some instances of biker gangs themselves prescribing to neo-Nazi ideology.

A History of Hell's Angels

This book is primarily about one of the most violent turf wars between biker gangs since the invention of the biker subculture: the Quebec Biker War. This war was fought between two rival biker gangs regarding Quebec's extremely valuable drug trade. One of the two gangs that were involved in this war is called "Hell's Angels", and is the gang that, arguably, instigated the turf war by attempting to overthrow a rival gang through brute force.

Hell's Angels is, perhaps, the most iconic and widely recognized biker gang in the world. There are a number of reasons for this fact, one of the most important being that this gang has been featured in social media more than perhaps any other biker gang in the world. They have been depicted in film in a variety of ways.

The most common way in which they are depicted is surprisingly positive, especially considering the level of crime in which Hell's Angels and other biker gangs are involved. The positive portrayals of Hell's Angels in film usually depict them as being free spirited and loyal to one another, depicting the gang as a sort of brotherhood rather than a criminal organization. Hell's Angels public image as a charitable organization has been a huge influence on their portrayal in the media.

This portrayal has become the iconic image of the gang, and is part of the reason why many people are entirely unaware that Hell's Angels is actually a gang of criminals and not a band of brothers who have sworn loyalty to one another. There are certain films that depict Hell's Angels along with other biker gangs in their true negative light, a prominent example being "*The Wild Angels*" which shows members of the gang to be ruthless criminals.

As for the gang itself, its members maintain that they are no more than simple motorcycle enthusiasts who come together to share their love of all things that have to do with motorcycles. They state that their innocent motives are clear based on the activities they undertake which range from parties to motorcycle rallies. They also often undertake charitable initiatives such as driving long distances to raise awareness for charitable causes or hosting fundraisers for charities.

As for the criminal element that is so often associated with Hell's Angels, the general response of a member to such an accusation would be that the criminal acts are conducted by the individuals themselves acting of their own free will and are not influenced by Hell's Angels or its ideology.

But law enforcement agencies consider Hell's Angels to be a criminal organization, and the widespread belief is that these charitable events are no more than covers to maintain a positive image for the gang so that they are able to undertake their criminal activities without having to worry about people watching out for them.

In order to understand their importance in the Quebec Biker War, it is important to first understand where the Hell's Angels come from, as this can greatly help one understand their underlying purpose.

Understanding the history of Hell's Angels will also give you an idea of what kind of criminal activities they are involved in, and what events led to the war that ended up taking so many lives in Quebec.

The Origins of Hell's Angels

There are so many different origin stories that have been spread around for this gang that it has become extremely difficult to ascertain just when and where Hell's Angels began. The reason for this confusion is partially the fact that many different biker gangs calling themselves Hell's Angels popped up at the same time in the same general geographic area, which means that nobody really knows which particular Hell's Angels was the original or if these different gangs were related. As far as most people could tell, these separate gangs did not interact with each other all that much.

But, there are certain aspects of the origins of Hell's Angels that can be said for sure. One aspect of the gang's origins is that it began in or around Fontana, California in 1948. ([9]) Although it is uncertain if this is the exact year in which Hell's Angels was created, most sources and evidence tends to point to this year.

The post-war period in which the gang came into being says a lot about why the gang was created in the first place. First and foremost, motorcycles were available at extremely cheap rates due to the fact that the market had a surplus of the vehicles following the end of the war. This meant that their popularity rose significantly after the war ended, and the philosophical connections that certain parties made between the motorcycle and the freedom of the open road resulted in the creation of a lot of biker gangs.

These biker gangs, particularly Hell's Angels, were populated mostly by war veterans. These war veterans were usually quite young, as the war had required a large number of youths to facilitate the massive scale of the military operations that were being conducted. When these young men returned home, they did so having been conditioned to tension, action and, most of all, adrenaline rushes on a daily basis.

The pallidness of post-war life left many of them restless. This is what led to a large number of them purchasing motorcycles, mostly due to the fact that the vehicle was considered to be dangerous and risky to operate. Many of these vets, whose personalities had been shaped by a highly idealized military experience, began to take out their aggression through these motorcycles and formed clubs and gangs. One of these veterans was a man named Otto Friedli, ([10]) a resident of Fontana, California.

Otto Friedli was a member of a biker gang called the *"Pissed Off Bastards"*. But, following a feud and some tension with fellow gang members, Friedli broke away from his biker gang to form his own gang, which he called *"Hell's Angels"* after the name of a squadron of fighter planes that became famous for its heroic exploits during the war. The fame of this squadron of fighter planes might explain why so many veterans that started biker gangs decided to name their gang after it as it exemplified the epitome of heroism during the war.

Friedli is very important in the history of the modern Hell's Angels as it is his club that eventually turned into the Hell's Angels that is so widely recognized today. He managed to procure longevity for his particular club because he was able to merge his biker gang into another similarly sized biker gang and thus became the major biker presence in the San Francisco area. His gang's domination of such a significant part of the most heavily populated state in the United States of America gave him much influence and allowed him to mold a legacy that has lived on to this day.

Part of the reason why Hell's Angels in particular became such a popular motorcycle club was the fact that it steeped itself in exclusivity and an air of mystery. Only members of the club knew what exactly happened in Hell's Angels-owned establishments, and becoming a member was, and is to this day, a notoriously difficult and time-consuming process. This made all motorcycle enthusiasts, along with the criminal element they were involved in, very interested in Hell's Angels, thus contributing to the club's enduring popularity.

Move Towards Crime

Although originally little more than a club for motorcycle aficionados, the members of Hell's Angels quickly got a reputation for being rowdy and violent, a reputation gained largely from the wild parties they would throw. When exactly the club moved towards intentionally committing illegal activities is not known, but at some point in the late 1950s or early 1960s, the presence of biker gangs, especially Hell's Angels, was beginning to be felt.

It was in the 1960s when the Hell's Angels began to receive widespread attention, in doing so becoming the first ever biker gang to truly get any major attention from media outlets. Hell's Angels, and biker gangs in general, represented subculture and, more importantly, counterculture. Counterculture was becoming increasingly popular, and the biker subculture maintained its own niche, maintaining its status as a subculture as the hippie movement, psychedelia and other popular countercultural movements slowly became a part of zeitgeist.

Apart from the pure counterculture vibe that Hell's Angels presented, a series of violent events committed by members of Hell's Angels in the 1960s also brought the biker gang into public view, particularly the more negative aspect of the gang's activities. Possibly the most well known of these violent actions by members of Hell's Angels was an incident that occurred during a Rolling Stones concert in 1969 when members of the gang assaulted several people and killed one. The gang allegedly planned to kill the front man and vocalist of the Rolling Stones, Mick Jagger, following the bad press that they received as a result of this incident.

The major violent incidents that occurred in the history of Hell's Angels had to do with turf wars, much like the Quebec Biker War which is the subject of this book. The violence wreaked during these turf wars was so severe that it prompted federal as well as local law enforcement agencies to begin considering Hell's Angels as an organized crime syndicate instead of a simple motorcycle appreciation club.

Hell's Angels is possibly the single most popular biker gang, or motorcycle club as they like to refer to themselves, in the world. There are chapters, or autonomous branches, of the

Hell's Angels gang in over fifty countries, with the total number of chapters amounting to well over four hundred. With each charter having around twenty-five members at least, this would mean that the worldwide membership of Hell's Angels probably exceeds ten thousand.

The presence of a veritable army of members of a criminal gang well known for its violence and aggression has resulted in a lot of distress for law enforcement, distress which is justified considering how much damage the gang has done in its frequent gang wars.

Characteristics of the Gang

As with all other biker gangs, Hell's Angels have a distinctive style of dressing that is designed to help its members stand apart from the crowd and publicly announce their membership of the gang with their very presence. The vest that is the traditional uniform of the member of any biker gang is usually accompanied by a variety of patches, with different patches meaning different things.

The true meaning behind these patches is not known, nor is it known what purpose the patches serve or what they are supposed to signify. But it has been frequently hypothesized that the patches represent the achievements of the member in question. In this way, the patches would be similar to the badges that are earned by Boy Scouts. The exact activities that would earn the member a patch are unknown, as is so much else about the gang. But it is probably safe to assume that the activities that win patches in an organization with a reputation such as Hell's Angels are probably not all that wholesome in nature.

Another extremely important aspect of the gang's overall image is the bikes that they choose to ride. The vast majority of Hell's Angels members ride bikes manufactured by Harley-Davidson. There are several reasons for this. The first of these reasons is that Harley-Davidson was one of only two companies to survive the recession, meaning that there were practically no other alternatives. They were also producing cheaper bikes, although this changed later on, meaning that veterans with little money could easily afford them.

The second reason that Hell's Angels members are so fond of Harley-Davidson bikes is that, in general, the biker subculture has a nationalist streak to it. This means that members of Hell's Angels would prefer products that are made in America to products that are made anywhere else. Hence, since Harley-Davidson is the only motorcycle company that manufactures the products it sells in America within America itself, it is naturally going to be favored heavily by members of Hell's Angels.

The gang also has a history of racial closed-mindedness. Although they state that they do not discriminate based on race, membership has often been reserved for white males only, with several members of the gang stating that they believe that the prime candidate for membership in the gang is a strong white male. But, as compared to other biker gangs, Hell's Angels is actually quite progressive when it comes to race.

The racial tension in the gang is more out of discomfort than actual belief in superiority of race. Although this discomfort itself is not exactly progressive, it displays a mentality that is at least slightly more advanced than that of other biker gangs, particularly those that exhibit full-fledged Nazi-like tendencies and believe in the superiority of the white race.

The general consensus on racial diversity within the organization is that the organization itself is not racist. It does not incorporate racist ideology into its practices nor does it officially require its members to be white. But the members of the gang are, more often than not, racist people and will thus not allow people of other races to join their ranks. Racial tension between white and black criminals has also resulted in black bikers creating their own gangs, such as the East Bay Dragons, which do not allow white bikers to join their ranks.

But, despite the racism of most of its members, Hell's Angels has been known to associate with black bikers, something that a lot of biker gangs would simply not do. One of the most important black bikers that Hell's Angels associated with was a man by the name of Gregory Wooley who served as the bodyguard of Maurice Boucher, one of the leaders of Hell's Angels during the Quebec turf war against Bandidos.

Membership Process

The process of becoming a member of Hell's Angels is notoriously difficult. Not only does the process take an inordinate amount of time, several years in fact, but becoming a proper fully inducted member requires every single member of that charter to vote that the applicant deserves to be in the gang and receive full membership.

There are certain requirements ([11]) that an applicant has to fulfill before he can even apply for membership. These requirements are the possession of a valid driver's license, possession of a motorcycle over 750cc as well as certain distinct personal qualities.

Exactly what personal qualities are required of Hell's Angels members is uncertain. But it is probably safe to assume that the qualities would involve a general aura of manliness and a fearless attitude since these personality traits are highly prized within the biker subculture.

Additionally, based on the criminal activities that Hell's Angels are involved in, trustworthiness during a criminal caper is probably going to be an important aspect of a prospective member's personality, as will be respect for superior or older members of the gang.

Also, since Hell's Angels is an extremely secretive organization, they would probably require the person to be trustworthy before allowing him to join the organization. Only allowing in members who are capable of keeping secrets is probably the only thing that has allowed the club to maintain its mysterious reputation for so long.

Police officers and anybody who has any ties to any form of law enforcement are not allowed to join for obvious reasons. Having members of the police force within the gang would create a conflict of interest, and such people would more often than not be informants for the police department who are attempting to bring the organization down somehow. Additionally, women are not allowed to be members, and are in many ways less desirable to Hell's Angels than men of different ethnicity. Hell's Angels firmly conform to the belief that women are weak and only good for deriving pleasure from, which means that there has never been a female member of the gang.

If the person that wants to join the gang fulfills all of the requirements, they move on to the next stage of acquiring membership. In this next phase, the potential member goes through a series of tests and trials. Although the tests and trials are unknown, they obviously involve seeing if the potential member has what it takes to take part in the criminal activities that the group is known for.

If the potential member successfully gets through this trial phase, they become partial members of the group known as a "Hang-around" within the organization and have very few of the member-related privileges. But they are allowed to come to certain club events and to meet members of the organization at club-owned venues after receiving special permission.

The Hang-around phase allows the potential member to ascertain whether the activities of the gang interest him or not. If he feels that he would not be able to fit in with the rest of the members of the gang, he can choose to end the process right there and not become a full member. But, if the potential member is interested, and if he is deemed worthy by the members, he gets promoted to what is known as a "Prospect". Prospects have all of the benefits of full members except for the fact that they do not get voting privileges and they are not allowed to wear patches yet.

Following this elevation to the rank of Prospect, the potential member has to win the vote of every single member of the charter that he wishes to join. This often involves a great deal of legwork, with the potential member having to meet every single member of the charter so that they can get to know him and raise any concerns that they might have with him. If he is able to win the support of every single member of the charter, a formal voting process will ensue and the Prospect will have to affirm his loyalty to the gang and its cause.

Once he becomes a full member, he is given his first patch along with the Hell's Angels insignia to sew onto his vest. He also becomes eligible to earn more patches by participating in the club's illicit activities and making a name for himself by being diligent in his club-related duties.

Full members are referred to as being "patched" members of the gang, and the process of becoming a patched member is often referred to as getting patched. The lengthy and difficult process ensures that only the most like-minded people would join the gang, thereby contributing to the ideological solidity of the gang and its members.

The patches that the member receives never become the member's property. If the member is ejected from the gang or if he chooses to leave, he must return the patches as they are still the property of the gang. This helps to preserve the sanctity of the logo and patches that the gang has created for itself, something which it also protects fiercely with a legal team in order to prevent their insignia being used on toys or any form of clothing.

An interesting fact to note is that once an individual becomes a Prospect, they are, for all intents and purposes, members of the gang. They take part in the gang's illicit activities, attend the vast majority of club-related events and become involved in turf wars and struggles for dominance of the drug trade.

This means that although the number of patched members of Hell's Angels is around ten thousand worldwide, the number of members both patched and prospective is closer to twenty thousand. Additionally, in some instances, Hang-arounds are also considered to be members, which would bring the total number of people who associate with the criminal network that is Hell's Angels to be almost forty thousand, although only a quarter of these have been patched.

History of Bandidos

There were two major players in the struggle for turf that became the Quebec Biker War, as has been mentioned previously. One of these players was obviously Hell's Angels. The other major player is another widely feared 1%er biker gang that calls itself "Bandidos".

Although Bandidos does not enjoy the heavy depiction in popular culture that Hell's Angels does, the gang is still widely feared for being brutal, aggressive and inordinately stubborn when it comes to their territory. As you will learn later in the book, the aggressive protective streak that this band possesses regarding their territory was a major contributing factor in the Quebec Biker War, along with Hell's Angels aggressive expansionist policies.

Bandidos is not as old as Hell's Angels, being created around two decades after the more famous gang. The gang does not have the sort of reputation that Hell's Angels have, although this changed somewhat after the Quebec Biker War. The history of Bandidos is far less murky than that of Hell's Angels, and their genesis can be traced back to a single creator.

Bandidos originated ([12]) in March of the year 1966 by a man named Donald Chambers. Chambers was greatly inspired by the outpouring of counterculture and subculture in the sixties and was particularly taken by the fact that the Beatles supported the legal variety of biker culture.

He was a dockworker at the time and, at thirty-six, was thoroughly frustrated with his life. He had always had a fondness for motorcycles and decided to act on this fondness by starting a biker gang. The motorcycle was one of two of his great passions, the other great passion being the second thing that influenced the overall culture of Bandidos.

This second passion of his was a passion for old western films. His favorite characters in these films were not the cowboys or even the Native Americans, referred to in the films as Indians. Instead, his favorite characters were the Mexican bandits that often served as alternate antagonists that the cowboys had to fight against.

Bandits in Spanish is *bandidos*, which is where Chambers got the inspiration for the name of his biker gang. He was greatly inspired by the free-spirited nature of the bandits in the films, especially the fact that they did what they wanted when they wanted to do it. This was an attitude that he admired and greatly wanted to implement in his own life.

It turned out to be an attitude that became pervasive in the ideology of Bandidos, and it helped turn their gang into an iconic part of the world of biker gangs. Indeed, the iconoclasm of Bandidos grew to the point where they rivaled Hell's Angels in some places, and they did all of that without the pop culture references to their gang.

The creation of the club coincided with the start of the Vietnam War. You already know from previous chapters that war veterans, especially the young ones who are drafted, get used to the lifestyle and are then sent home, are often discontented with post-war life. Hence, when the war finished, Bandidos saw its numbers swell as a large number of Vietnam War veterans decided to join the gang in order to get some excitement in their post-war lives.

Following the swelling of the club's numbers in the 1970s after the end of the Vietnam War, the operations of Bandidos expanded, and they were able to secure a large piece of the drug trade in many areas. The most significant of these areas was in Montreal, Quebec. With Bandidos being a relatively young gang, and Hell's Angels having an older and prouder culture as well as a general superiority complex, a clash was going to happen one way or another. This was one of the most significant contributing factors to the eruption of the Quebec Biker War.

Membership and Criminal Activities

Although it does not have an international membership that is as extensive as that of Hell's Angels, Bandidos does have over two hundred chapters in almost two dozen countries with thousands of patched members. The wide variety of countries in which they have established their operations in means that they have a lot of firepower and are often second only to Hell's Angels themselves as far as the authorities go.

The main country in which Bandidos is established is, of course, the United States of America. Whereas Hell's Angels originate from California, Bandidos found its origins further down south in the state of Texas, specifically in the city of Houston. It has always been concentrated mostly in the southern states of America, but over the course of its history, it gradually progressed northwards before it finally reached Canada.

Currently, Bandidos has a presence in Louisiana, Missouri, Mississippi, Alabama, Arkansas, New Mexico, Colorado, Washington, Montana, South Dakota, Utah, Idaho, Wyoming, Nevada, Oklahoma, and Nebraska along with smaller operations in several other states. As far as Canada goes, Bandidos has enjoyed a sizeable presence in Montreal and Toronto, particularly after they began working with Canadian biker gang Rock Machine.

The criminal activities ([13]) that Bandidos has taken part in within North America are numerous and diverse. The most popular area of criminal activity is, obviously, the main illegal activity that they take part in. Much like most other biker gangs, the main drug that Bandidos trades in is Crystal meth. Bandidos is unique among biker gangs in that they manufacture and fence the meth themselves, and even sell it on the street level. This was what made them so successful in Montreal and what prompted Hell's Angels to begin attacking them in order to reclaim the extremely valuable drug territory that they had begun to lose.

Bandidos also enjoys a sizable presence in Australia, although its presence in New Zealand is still restricted to about a dozen members operating out of a single chapter. Their criminal activities within Australia have been extremely violent, and their tendency to enter into turf wars with rival gangs has resulted in a bloody war with the gang

Comanchero, a war that ended up costing over a dozen lives before it was over. The truly heart-breaking aspect of these deaths is the fact that, though most of the people killed were members of one gang or the other, one of the victims was an innocent fourteen-year-old boy.

Apart from this shootout incident, there have been several other isolated instances where members of Bandidos opened fire in public along with several police raids on drug warehouses and illegal weapon storage facilities which have implicated members of Bandidos through the evidence that was discovered. Although most of these incidences did not result in anyone's death, the fact remains that Bandidos members create a climate of danger wherever they are present.

Additionally, the club's presence is significant in France as well as Germany, although they have not been involved in violent activity in these countries as much as they have in North America and Australia. Bear in mind however, that this statement that Bandidos members in these countries are not as violent as other chapters in the world is a comparative statement. There have been two instances where members of Bandidos were accused of murder. Additionally, a rogue faction of Turkish members of Bandidos started a three-month-long war with members of Hell's Angels, adding just another notch to the number of altercations between these two rival gangs.

The Bandidos chapters that exist in Scandinavia have been extremely violent and aggressive in their drug trafficking, being involved in a turf war so bloody and destructive that it is referred to as the Great Nordic Biker War. It is interesting to note that this turf war was also fought against Hell's Angels. This violence is somewhat endemic to Bandidos' presence in Scandinavia, and is also a big part of Bandidos drug culture in the Netherlands, as well.

Ever since the club opened its very first charter in the Netherlands it has been under surveillance by Dutch law enforcement officials operating at both federal as well as local levels. As a result, the Dutch chapters of Bandidos have been unable to cause any real damage, but they were involved in bombing the car of a noted Dutch politician who was working on eradicating biker culture from the Netherlands.

Additionally, a raid conducted on a Bandidos-owned venue uncovered the presence of heavy weaponry, including fifteen rocket launchers. It is unknown what exactly the gang was planning on doing with those rocket launchers, but finding them in time probably prevented one of the worst gang assaults in the history of 1%er biker culture.

Bandidos' involvement in the drug trade has naturally led to a great deal of violence as well in the countries it has been established in. All in all, at least over a hundred people have been killed by Bandidos members directly so far, with at least a hundred more having been killed due to the repercussions of the turf wars that Bandidos had a tendency to get into.

Members have also been involved in a lot of violence that is separate from the drug trade, violence that seems frivolous and done for the fun of it more than anything else. As with all other 1%er gangs, Bandidos members claim that the crimes are the work of the individuals and have absolutely nothing to do with the ideology of the gang in any way. Whatever the case may be, the evidence proves that wherever there is a significant

Bandidos presence, violence is not just a possibility, it is an inevitability.

Characteristics of Bandidos

Hell's Angels is defined by symbolism that pertains to death and hellish afterlife scenarios. Angelic symbolism is also used, often being juxtaposed against the hellish symbolism in a manner that is ironic as well as sinister. But, with Bandidos, the symbolism that is used in their imagery, and particularly their logo, is completely different. ([14])

Since Chambers was a huge fan of Mexican bandits, imagery pertaining to Mexican outlaws is heavily prevalent among the Bandidos. The logo of the gang itself is a cartoonish image of a Mexican outlaw, similar to the depictions of Mexican outlaws that were popularized by the popular cartoon show, Looney Tunes, in the 1960s and 1970s.

The patches and vest, along with other aspects of biker attire and accouterments, are all similar to a large extent to the vast majority of biker gangs. Long beards, sunglasses, caps and tattoos are all a big part of the way members of Bandidos present themselves, and masculinity is a huge part of Bandidos ideology.

But, an important difference between the ideology of Bandidos and practically every other biker gang in the world is that they are significantly more tolerant as far as race is concerned. The name itself is inspired by Mexico, and the gang actually reflects the love of Mexican culture in their wide acceptance of Latino individuals into their gang. Indeed, if it had not been for Bandidos, the concept of a

Mexican biker, a concept now widely accepted and featured in films, might never have come to exist.

This acceptance of other races and ethnicities is not just restricted to Latinos. International chapters of Bandidos are also significantly more accepting of potential members from other ethnics than the vast majority of biker gangs in the world. The German chapters of Bandidos accept Turkish immigrants into their ranks. Considering the highly racist ideology that permeates German society, the fact that Turkish immigrants are accepted in any German institution is incredible, but the fact that the institution that accepts them is a biker gang is often considered to be too outlandish to believe.

This acceptance of non-Mexican members is part of the reason that Bandidos was able to enjoy such a meteoric rise and come to rival older and better established gangs such as Hell's Angels. Additionally, this culture of acceptance within Bandidos made its members fiercely loyal to the gang, as they had found through it a place where they belonged and were accepted for who they were, in essence, a place where they could be themselves. The institution that is the Bandidos Motorcycle Club might actually be worthy of admiration if it wasn't involved in so much violence and trafficking of illegal substances.

But, what is true for other biker gangs is also true, at least to some extent, for Bandidos as well. Hell's Angels, for example, is not a racist organization, at least officially. But their members are extremely racist, which means that the gang often exhibits racist behavior and commits acts of race-related violence. Similarly, Bandidos is an organization that is not ideologically racist in and of itself. In fact, it prides itself on being a very racially diverse organization and how that makes it different and better than other biker gangs that do not allow members of other ethnics to join. Despite this, members of Bandidos have been known to be racist.

This often causes tension within the gang, as white supremacist members clash with members of the gang that belong to different ethnicities. The tension in the gang caused by such occurrences often causes violence to spill over and splinter groups to form. The majority of Bandidos have been known to be opposed to gay marriage, mostly due to the fact that homosexuality goes against the biker's glorification of the ubermensch and the desire among all members of biker gangs to appear as macho and masculine as possible.

The presence of individual members with racist tendencies does not usually cause friction great enough to cause actual rifts between the members of the group. After all, the gang has been active for half a century now and has been able to stand up to Hell's Angels, a gang with almost twice its number of members. It would not have been able to do this if it was constantly being hampered by racial tensions within its ranks. The tension exists but is often tolerated for the sake of the gang, and races often work together to this end.

It should be noted that, no matter how accepting Bandidos is of members of races other than white, it does not allow female members. The vast majority of Bandidos chapters do not allow female bikers to become patched members, although a small minority do allow women to get to levels equal to that of Prospects. The misogynistic viewpoint that women are weak and only serve a purpose as objects men can derive pleasure from is just as pervasive in Bandidos as it is in every other biker gang, which just goes to show that a 1%er will never be anything more than a 1%er.

Support Clubs

Bandidos is also well known for frequently using what are known as support clubs. ([15]) These support clubs are smaller biker gangs that operate autonomously but are loyal to Bandidos. If one were to use an analogy to better understand how support clubs work, members of Bandidos are lords and members of support clubs are their vassals.

Support clubs serve a variety of purposes. The most important purpose that support clubs serve is that they are able to provide legal fronts that Bandidos can use to launder its money. Since Bandidos is now widely known to be involved in illicit activities, any property or business that the club owns itself will be under intense scrutiny.

This means that any businesses that Bandidos attempts to open in order to launder the money that it receives from its illegal activities would be rendered useless because law enforcement authorities would be constantly examining the financial affairs of the business. Hence, such front businesses become little more than ways to earn clean money that can be used for funding Bandidos activities and pay members without raising suspicion.

But, in order to facilitate the laundering of the large amounts of money that Bandidos earns through its drug dealings, it needs legal organizations that can open its businesses for it. This is where support clubs come in. Since support clubs are not under as much scrutiny as Bandidos, indeed some of them being practically invisible to law enforcement officials, it is very easy for them to open businesses and launder money through said businesses.

Another important function that support clubs serve is to perform illegal activities on behalf of Bandidos. Often, the heat on the gang is far too great to allow it to conduct drug deals or to fight turf wars. Support clubs can get the job done for the gang, and they are also extremely useful in turf wars. Having support clubs gives Bandidos access to a lot of manpower without having to hand out memberships to everybody that is about to fight in the war.

These clubs do things for Bandidos in exchange for the prestige and safety that comes with being associated with such a famous and well-respected biker gang, and Bandidos gets a larger army of soldiers and helpers for the variety of tasks that it undertakes. They are an important part of why Bandidos, despite having half the manpower that Hell's Angels possesses, were able to stand up to possibly the single most powerful biker gang in the world on three separate occasions in three different countries.

A lot of biker gangs now apply the concept of support clubs, simply due to the fact that they are extremely useful. But, Bandidos is the gang that pioneered the concept in the first place, thus proving that the gang is a lot more dangerous than it looks because it has the brains to match the brawn.

The Quebec Turf War

One of the bloodiest and most destructive turf wars in the history of 1% biker gangs was the *Quebec Biker War*. The scale of the war itself, the number of players involved, the damage that was caused along with how much money and territory was at stake all came together to set the stakes very high for this war.

You are already aware and informed about the two major gangs that fought the war. It is now time to understand just what they were fighting for, and what circumstances led to the war in the first place.

It must be noted that well before the war even started, Hell's Angels was having a difficult time consolidating its position in Canada. The gang has never been able to enter the country in full force for some reason, but there was no reason for the higher level members of the gang to really worry about this. After all, there was nobody who was powerful or brave enough to take on Hell's Angels, particularly after the brutal and aggressive image that they had created for themselves since their inception along with the vast numbers of its members.

But, well before the turf war even began, there were several instances that indicated that Hell's Angels was losing what little grip it had on its Canadian territory. The main reason for this instability in Canadian chapters of Hell's Angels was enmity between chapters in the south of Canada and chapters in the north. The southern members considered their northern counterparts to be too wild and suspected them of cheating the rest of the chapters out of profits that they were owed, based on the system of equal distribution that dictated that all chapters would receive a basic payment which would be supplemented by commissions on sales.

It is true that members of northern Canadian Hell's Angels chapters were far less responsible about their duties than they should have been. This is most likely the result of a lack of competition leading to complacency. Members of these northern chapters often consumed the drugs that they were supposed to sell, and often did cut into profits that were owed to chapters in the south of Canada. Basic payments aside, members of northern Canadian chapters were cutting into commission on the sales southern chapters were making as well, something southern

Canadian Hell's Angels members obviously found to be completely unacceptable.

These occurrences were actually exacerbating a preexisting enmity that occurred as the result of the jobs that specific chapters were assigned, these assignments being indicative of the poor organization of the Canadian Hell's Angels chapters. Southern Canadian chapters were the manufacturing hubs - they were the ones who manufactured the bulk of the meth that was sold throughout Canada. Half of this meth was sent up north to fellow chapters so that they could sell it. The northern chapters held a large portion of the money that was made and so were responsible for the distribution of funds.

When funds began to run low, southern chapters began to speculate that their northern brothers were eating the profits. It was discovered through an internal audit that northern members had actually stolen $96,000 that was owed to the Nunavut chapter. This was proof that money was being stolen. In order to fix this situation, the charter in Quebec decided to take action and put a stop to the rogue northern chapter once and for all.

On March 24, 1985, five senior north members were invited to Lennoxville to meet with the Quebec-based Hell's Angels members. When these northern Hell's Angels members arrived, they were shot to death and their bodies were stuffed into plastic bags and thrown into the St. Lawrence River with weights attached.

The repercussions of this event, which would eventually come to be known as the Lennoxville Massacre, ([16]) were severe and widespread. It can be argued that the first stirrings of the eventual turf war began here, in spite of the fact that Bandidos were nowhere near powerful enough to take on Hell's Angels at this point.

This event can be said to have caused the eventual turf war because it was the initial stone in the previously serene lake that caused the ripples that would eventually lead to the violence in Quebec. These ripples were numerous, but perhaps the most significant was a direct result of the fact that high-ranking Hell's Angels members from the Quebec charter were the ones who did the deed.

Eventually the bodies were found and it did not take law enforcement very long to connect the assassinations to four high-ranking members of Hell's Angels. Harold Pelletier, Luc "Sam" Michaud, Réjean "Zig-Zag" Lessard, and Robert "Snake" Tremblay were convicted of first-degree murder and sentenced to 25 years in prison. They have all since been granted parole.

These killings created a vacuum in the upper ranks of the organization and were the first of the two major ripples caused by the Lennoxville Massacre.

The second major ripple was the fact that this act was considered extreme even in the criminal underworld. Several members of Hell's Angels found this to be an act so intense that it resulted in a line being crossed, a line that they could now never cross back over. This created discontent among the members of Hell's Angels within Canada, something that would play an important role in the war to come.

New Management

Following the disastrous aftermath of the Lennoxville Massacre, Hell's Angels chapters in Canada desperately needed a new leader. They found one in a man named Maurice "Mom" Boucher, ([17]) someone who was instrumental in the upcoming turf war.

The discontent in the group also had its own consequences. A strong-willed member of the gang by the name of Salvatore Cazzetta ([18]) decided that Hell's Angels was no longer for him and broke away from the group. He created his own small biker gang called Rock Machine. As you will discover later on in this book, Rock Machine would prove to be an important part of the turf war to come.

Maurice Boucher was tasked with salvaging what was left of the Montreal Hell's Angels. The chapter had created a bad reputation for itself after the Lennoxville Massacre and so had to deal with bad relations with practically every criminal element in Canada, including fellow chapters of Hell's Angels. This obviously made Boucher's difficult job practically impossible to do. Boucher also had to deal with Rock Machine, particularly the fact that a member of his own chapter was able to so blatantly go against everything that the gang stood for and make his own splinter group without facing any consequences. This problem was compounded by the fact that Rock Machine was becoming a thorn in the side of his chapter by competing with them for a section of the drug market in Montreal. Although this section that they had apportioned for themselves was small, it was biting into the already dwindling profits of the Canadian chapters of Hell's Angels.

Boucher clearly had to make an example out of Cazzetta, as well as Rock Machine, if he was going to ensure the longevity of his operation and secure his future as a leading member of Hell's Angels. But he was faced with a significant roadblock in this endeavor, one that would end up playing a major role in delaying the inevitable turf war.

This roadblock had to do with the fact that Cazzetta was connected to the Italian mafia in Quebec. There are very few Italian members of Hell's Angels, which meant that Cazzetta was a major exception and something of an oddity, especially in the Canadian Hell's Angels chapters.

But his Italian heritage could not stop him from becoming a member of Hell's Angels because of his connections with one of the most powerful criminal organizations in Canada and the major crime syndicate controlling criminal activities within Quebec. Cazzetta's connection to the Quebec mafia also made him immune to any threats from Boucher.

In order to understand why Boucher was reluctant to threaten Cazzetta because of his connections to the Italian mafia, you have to understand just how powerful the mafia was at the time. They were so powerful that going up against them would result in an extremely devastating war.

Since the Montreal chapter of Hell's Angels was already in danger of collapsing in the wake of the Lennoxville Massacre, going up against the Quebec mafia was not something that Boucher could afford to do. He could not even rely on help from other Hell's Angels chapters in Canada because of the low reputation that his chapter now had after murdering members of its own gang. Hence, with so few resources and no friends to help him fight the war, going up against the Quebec mafia would have resulted in the Montreal chapter of Hell's Angels potentially getting wiped out completely.

For a long while, Hell's Angels and Rock Machine coexisted relatively peacefully. Boucher did not want to upset the Quebec mafia, and Cazzetta was unwilling to take part in any wars himself, the reasons for which you will see in the next section.

Salvatore Cazzetta (above)

Maurice Boucher (above)

Various Threats to Rock Machine

On the other side of the coin, although Rock Machine was insulated from any threat that Hell's Angels posed, they were not exactly a powerful power gang on their own. People could not touch Cazzetta because he was related to several prominent members of the Quebec mafia, but the protection only extended to Cazzetta himself.

As for members of his gang, they were easy pickings for larger biker gangs looking to make a mark and consolidate territory. These gangs had been unable to do this previously since the territory now held by Rock Machine used to be property of Hell's Angels. Attempting to procure said territory would have resulted in practically every chapter of Hell's Angels in Quebec coming down upon them with a fury that would have wiped their entire organization off of the face of the map.

But this territory was now owned by Rock Machine, an independent gang with a low membership rate and absolutely no support from any other part of the country. This meant that larger gangs saw the opportunity to expand their own territory by taking down the nascent Rock Machine. All they would have to do is ensure that Cazzetta himself was not harmed and that they left a little something for Cazzetta to live off of.

The Italian mafia in Quebec would not have forgiven any gang that would have left a member of their family destitute. They would have eliminated any criminal element that brought any physical harm to Cazzetta or his family. But, if they managed, through turf war and offensive strategies, to force Cazzetta into a retreat or surrender, they would be able to take his turf without having to face the Quebec mafia.

This is because of the intricate complexities of the honor code among criminals. Cazzetta was responsible for his own criminal operation. Although his relatives in the mafia would always ensure that he had a source of income and that there would never be any threat to his own safety or the safety of his family, Cazzetta alone was responsible for the success of his criminal endeavor. Therefore, forcing him into surrender would allow the gang that succeeded in doing this to take over his turf without incurring the wrath of the mafia.

This honor code is partly the reason why even forcing Cazzetta into surrendering his territory was not an option for Boucher or Hell's Angels. Hell's Angels, at least the Montreal chapter, had broken the biggest rule in any criminal's honor code: never kill your own. If Boucher even tried to take the territory that Rock Machine had, the mafia would come down hard simply because they didn't like the way that Hell's Angels did things.

Coming back to Rock Machine, as you can tell from the situation, Cazzetta had nothing to fear from Boucher or Hell's Angels, but he had his work cut out for him as far as consolidating his position and defending his interest from other gangs in the area went. He simply did not possess the manpower or the firepower to be able to stand up to several of the larger gangs in the area. To make matters worse, the smaller gangs that Rock Machine would have been able to take individually had started to band together in order to take the valuable territory from Rock Machine.

These small gangs did not control much territory, no more than a corner or two apiece. But, by cooperating, they would have been able to double their territory and thus their income.

Many of these smaller gangs coming together meant that Cazzetta's position and his turf was under major threat. These were the first major stirrings of the turf war in Montreal. But, even if a turf war had erupted with all of these players, it would not have been all that notable. It would not have spread outside of this one section of Montreal. As it turned out, Cazzetta was able to prevent this minor biker war from erupting, thereby saving the area of Montreal that he held interests in from major destruction.

But the tactic he used in order to protect himself from the minor turf war actually set in motion the events that would eventually trigger a much larger war, one that would encompass all of Quebec and would result in more destruction than would ever have occurred if Cazzetta had just surrendered in the first place.

Rock Machine

Meanwhile, back to the Bandidos.

Bandidos was the major criminal element in Montreal's incredibly lucrative drug business before the war erupted. This may seem surprising to you, especially considering how powerful Hell's Angels was supposed to be. But you have to remember that Hell's Angels had always been weak in Canada before Boucher arrived on the scene. With infighting and rogue members plaguing the group, Hell's Angels chapters in Canada were never as threatening as their American counterparts.

As a result, Bandidos never really had any rivals as far as the drug trade was concerned. The Quebec mafia had their own scene and Bandidos had their own. There were collaborations, occasional violence, but for the most part, the two major criminal organizations seemed to coexist peacefully.

When Rock Machine broke away from Hell's Angels, Bandidos was one of the gangs that was interested in taking the prime territory they owned away from them. Indeed, it would have been incredibly easy to take over the territory that Rock Machine possessed because there was simply no other biker gang that would have been able to stand up to them.

But Bandidos was a lot smarter about the situation than most people gave them credit for. They saw in this situation not just an opportunity to gain valuable real estate that would greatly boost their profits in Montreal, but an opportunity to increase their influence and reputation as well.

Bandidos and Rock Machine

You have already been introduced to the concept of support clubs. Bandidos was one of the first major biker gangs to start taking up clubs and providing them with protection in exchange for getting favors and support from said clubs in their times of need.

Rock Machine was a small club at the time and had absolutely no one on its side. Bandidos saw this as an opportunity. Although the Quebec mafia would not have cared if any criminal organization took over Rock Machine's turf through respectable means, these means being forcing Cazzetta into surrendering or retreating, Bandidos realized that they could use this situation to get into the Quebec mafia's good graces.

The Quebec mafia would look very kindly upon any organization that would have helped their relative's endeavor in his time of need. Bandidos approached Rock Machine and offered support club status. This would protect Rock Machine and its territory from practically any threat that would look to take their turf from them, it would get Bandidos the support of the Quebec mafia, and it would get them a piece of prime real estate. In addition, Rock Machine would have to give Bandidos a cut of their profits in order to justify their status as support club-owned.

Cazzetta, seeing no other option, agreed to this deal. It must be noted that the deal involving a share of the profits was somewhat unusual, mostly due to the incredibly high percentage that Cazzetta agreed to give to Bandidos. Larger clubs usually offer a small percentage and ask for support during turf battles. Cazzetta agreed to a larger percentage than normal and also agreed to provide manpower and firepower to Bandidos if they should ever need it.

This shows just how desperate Cazzetta was to consolidate his position and ensure that no one would be able to take his territory from him. It also exhibits how smart the higher level members of Bandidos were in this situation, as they were able to get far more from it than anybody would have been able to guess.

The great collaboration between Bandidos and Rock Machine began. Rock Machine would eventually outgrow their status as a support club, but the fact that Bandidos took them under their wing would prove to be extremely profitable for them in the long run. The fact of the matter remains, the war was brewing quite obviously, and as you will read in the next section, Hell's Angels had not been idle while their enemies were forming alliances and consolidating their positions.

Hell's Angels Under Boucher

While Rock Machine allied with Bandidos and took control of their territory, Boucher was busy repairing the damage that had been caused to his club by its former leaders. This was an extremely difficult task, to say the least, but Boucher was not the sort of man who would back down from a challenge.

In order to understand what Hell's Angels did in the decade preceding the start of the war, one must first understand the various problems that they were faced with.

First and foremost, Hell's Angels had to get back what it had lost. The Lennoxville Massacre had left the gang weaker than ever before, not just because they lost their leaders but because they lost a huge chunk of valuable real estate as well to Rock Machine. They were also in danger of losing their various assets to opportunistic takeovers by rival gangs. Hell's Angels simply did not have the manpower to keep itself afloat in Montreal, and the reason for this is the second problem that Boucher faced.

The other problem that Boucher faced was that the Montreal chapter of Hell's Angels had to redeem itself in the eyes of its peers. Fellow Hell's Angels chapters in Canada looked at the Montreal chapter with mistrust, which meant that Boucher could not rely on them to help him regain his lost real estate, nor could he depend on them to help him keep his existing interests safe.

For all intents and purposes, the Montreal chapter of Hell's Angels was a lone biker gang, no more powerful than a support club. Even going head to head with Rock Machine, without the mafia support and at full Montreal manpower, would have been an extremely difficult undertaking in the current situation in which Boucher's chapter of the 1%ers biker gang found itself.

Boucher also had to prove himself. He had to do something big in order to win the respect of Hell's Angels chapters outside of Montreal. He had come in a time when Montreal-based Hell's Angels were looked down upon by practically every member of the organized crime community in Canada. Boucher had to prove himself and his gang to these criminals; otherwise, they would come together and take what was his out of spite simply because they didn't respect him. This was somewhat unfair, considering that Boucher had played no part in the Lennoxville Massacre or any of the other activities of Hell's Angels before he joined.

Another problem that Boucher faced involved proving himself to the more powerful American Hell's Angels. Canada had been a disappointment to the American chapters of Hell's Angels practically since their establishment in Canada. Boucher was responsible for the chapter that had caused the Americans the most embarrassment. But, if he wanted to protect the interests that he had, regain the turf he had lost, and expand Hell's Angels so that it had the same level of respect that it had in the US, he would need the support of the American Hell's Angels.

Boucher set off to repair the damage that had been caused. In the decade preceding the eruption of the Quebec Biker War in 1994, he visited all of the major chapters in Canada, starting with the north chapters, the members of which had been killed in the Lennoxville Massacre. Although his funds were low, Boucher took a gamble by offering to compensate the northern chapters for each member that they had lost. The money itself wasn't really enough to get him completely back into the good graces of the northern chapters, but it showed the other established Canadian Hell's Angels chapters that Boucher had a different way of doing things.

Apart from the north chapters, Boucher visited several of the west chapters of Hell's Angels as well. These chapters had been mostly separate from the rivalry between the northern and southern groups and looked upon their eastern counterparts with disdain. They were also an incredibly professional outfit, and thus were both the most profitable in Canada along with being the most powerful. Boucher would need their manpower if he wanted to consolidate his position and get the respect that he wanted.

After several years of treating them as though they were his lady lovers, the western chapters were firmly in support of Boucher and everything that he sought to do.

It is a testament to Boucher's intelligence that he did not simply go to the powerful chapters and be done with it. Instead, he went to the smaller chapters as well, ones with fewer members and lower profits.

Although in retrospect, many people state that Boucher treated them like support clubs rather than chapters of his own gang, Boucher very brilliantly was able to win the support of these smaller chapters by treating them with respect. As a result, he was able to call upon them when he needed their help. Although, separately, they did not have much manpower to make a huge difference, when they came together, their combined strength was enough to help Boucher greatly when the time came to go to war.

Boucher's final problem was manpower in his own camp. Although he was making his relationships with other chapters in Canada stronger, and these chapters would be willing to send him support when he needed it, his manpower within his own ranks was very thin. This was problematic for two reasons.

First and foremost, Boucher knew that if something happened and he needed people to fight for him, help would not be able to come from other chapters immediately. Even if he was able to send word out as quickly as possible to the nearest chapters, it would take them a few days at least to get a force together, arm themselves and get to Montreal in time.

During this wait for reinforcements, Boucher knew that what little forces he had would be decimated, and by the time reinforcements got there, there would simply be nothing left for them to save.

The second problem was that being low on manpower meant that his chapter was an easy target for any gang that wanted the territory that they possessed. Acquiring territory meant gaining higher ground, which meant that if a gang was powerful enough to take Boucher and his chapter down and gain his territory, they would have an advantage against reinforcements who would want to take the territory back for them.

An additional, but less immediate problem was that rival gangs would see that Hell's Angels members were pouring into the city, and they would take it as a sign that a war was coming, thereby giving them ample time to arm themselves and consolidate their forces before an actual attack occurred. In order to maintain the element of surprise, Boucher would need his own forces to be stronger than they were. He also would obviously need more men in order to expand his territory and improve the standing of Hell's Angels within Montreal.

In order to boost his ranks, Boucher became somewhat less strict about allowing members into the fold. Although it was still quite difficult for someone to become a proper patched member of Hell's Angels, Boucher made it easier for people to become Prospects. This was an intelligent move because it created for him an auxiliary force that he could use whenever he needed.

These Prospects would be desperate to prove themselves in order to merit them joining the group. Simply allowing people to become members would have diluted the purity of Hell's Angels memberships and would not have given these new members as much of a reason to fight as it would if they were Prospects looking to make an impression.

Boucher also obviously needed to increase his firepower. He had Hell's Angels leaders stockpile their weapons and ammunition in order to stay prepared for any potential attack from rivals.

This showed Boucher's cunning in a big way. Procuring large amounts of weaponry would have tipped off authorities that something dangerous and destructive was about to happen. No matter how discreet Boucher would have been, even so discreet that authorities would never have been able to link him to the large weapons acquisition that was going on, the phenomenon itself would have spooked authorities enough that they would start breaking down doors.

This could have led to a lot more problems for Boucher as he would have invariably ended up losing his entire stock of ammunition and weaponry and would have probably had to suffer losses in the manpower department as well as many of his men would have been arrested in connection with the illegal weaponry.

However, he was able to solidify his position and prepare himself for expansion. He had his job cut out for him but his position was helped by the fact that Quebec is one of the most profitable venues for the drug trade. Everybody in Canada wanted a piece of it, making it Boucher's primary bargaining chip. He was successfully able to leverage the prospect of gaining a major foothold with Quebec and thereby solved virtually every problem he had been facing after he had been elected as leader of the Montreal chapter of Hell's Angels.

Boucher's shrewd and crafty manner, in which he had made himself stronger without tipping off his enemies, won him a lot of support from the American Hell's Angels. This solved the last major problem that he had been facing, as gaining the support of American chapters meant that he had their help at his disposal. The US Hell's Angels were significantly more powerful than the Canadians', and winning their support strengthened Boucher's position immensely.

With all the pieces set on the board, the air was rife with tension. The war was about to begin.

***

Rock Machine and Bandidos were satisfied with their position in the months leading up to the war. Their partnership was profitable and, as far as they knew, their combined force was heads and shoulders above any other criminal element of the city, at least within the 1%er community. These two outlaw gangs enjoyed their prosperity before the war began. They had the largest share of the drug traffic after the mafia and were actually inching closer to owning just as much as the mafia did, which had actually started to create tension between Cazzetta and his mafioso relatives.

But the outbreak of the war caught them somewhat by surprise, particularly since they had no idea that Hell's Angels had been amassing in secret.

Cazzetta had been escalating his drug business after getting protection courtesy of Bandidos. Bandidos got a share of the drugs that he sold within his area, but Cazzetta wanted to up the ante by bringing more drugs into the country, drugs that only he would be selling. He was hoping that this would drive up demand and bring more traffic to his area.

Although biker gangs were still traditionally only selling meth, which was the only drug that they created, Cazzetta wanted to expand his product line. Montreal was still a production hub, but the production of meth was mostly in the hands of Bandidos and Hell's Angels. Rock Machine's status as support club meant that Cazzetta was provided with meth in exchange for providing a significant portion of the profits back to Bandidos. But Cazzetta resented this dependency on Bandidos and wanted to be able to provide something himself.

He branched out by procuring other drugs such as heroin and cocaine. This would eventually be the cause of his undoing, but for a time it proved to be extremely profitable. Bandidos had no claim to Cazzetta's cocaine, nor did they have any claim to the profits derived from said cocaine. Cazzetta was able to sell Bandidos cocaine, thereby providing him with independence from his protectors at least in a financial sense.

Soon, a significant portion of the criminal element in Montreal discovered that Cazzetta was bringing in cocaine that they could purchase, which meant that he became a supplier to a lot of gangs. This helped to erase a lot of the rivalries that existed between Rock Machine and other similarly sized gangs. This would prove to be very useful to Rock Machine during the war to come, but by that time it would be far too late for Cazzetta himself.

In order to understand the significance of Cazzetta becoming a supplier to what happened next, it is important that you understand the gravity of what being a supplier entails. Dealers are small-time criminals as far as law enforcement officials are concerned. They sell drugs but in amounts so small that arresting them doesn't do that much good, and there are far too many out there to capture all of them.

What law enforcement officials are truly interested in is cutting off the source, arresting the supplier in order to cut off the flow of drugs entirely. Although when Cazzetta became a supplier, he earned a lot more respect among his peers and began to profit a lot more from his criminal endeavors, he simultaneously painted a large bull's eye on his head for all of the authorities to see.

The huge influx of drugs was noted by the authorities after several drug dealers were arrested in possession of cocaine, the chemical signature for which had not been noted before within Montreal. This told authorities that there was a new supplier in town, and a coordinated task force was assembled for the purpose of taking this new supplier down. After a significant period of time, authorities gained enough information to point them to this new supplier.

Cazzetta was arrested at a pitbull farm he used to store his drugs. He was found with eleven tons of cocaine, an amount so large that it put Cazzetta away for decades, leaving a vacuum in the leadership of Rock Machine. This also finally gave Boucher his opportunity to strike, although Boucher, being the shrewd tactician that he was, chose not to strike immediately. Instead, he chose to be subtle. But the arrest of Cazzetta was an enormous blow to Rock Machine, and it finally gave Hell's Angels a way to enter into a turf war and potentially win back the ground that they had lost, along with expanding their territory immensely.

Subterfuge and the First Strike

After Cazzetta's arrest, Rock Machine went through a period of instability. Boucher took advantage of this by creating what came to be known as "puppet clubs". ([19])

Boucher was inspired in this endeavor by Bandidos, in particular their use of support clubs to do dirty work or expand territory. Boucher saw the importance of support clubs and decided to use them, except with a small twist. His clubs were formed of lesser-known members of his own gang, mostly Prospects, and they had one sole purpose: spread discontent within Rock Machine.

These puppet clubs went to Rock Machine-owned establishments and attempted to persuade the owners of these establishments that Rock Machine was finished and that there was no more profit to be had in the drug business. They attempted to persuade these people to sell off their interest to Hell's Angels.

Boucher's attempt at subterfuge showed that he knew the importance of not causing violence. No violence would mean that law enforcement officials would not get wind of a takeover going down, which meant that Boucher would be able to take over Rock Machine-owned establishments and territories without having to worry about the police breathing down his neck.

Another major situation that Boucher had to handle quickly had to do with Cazzetta's drug supply. Cazzetta was imprisoned, but the source that had been bringing the drugs into the country for him had not been apprehended. Additionally, many gangs and dealers within Montreal had become dependent on Cazzetta for their supply of drugs. They no longer had a supplier from whom they could procure cocaine and heroin.

This vacuum left in the Montreal drug trade was seen by Boucher to be an opportunity. Unfortunately for him, Bandidos saw this opportunity as well, which sparked a race of sorts for the drug supplier. This was one of the most important aspects of the events leading up to the war that ended up causing the war in the first place. The potential to become a supplier and to triple profits was too good of an opportunity to miss.

But Boucher's subterfuge, though brilliant, left a lot of Hell's Angels frustrated. With Cazzetta out of the way, Hell's Angels saw no reason not to go to war with Rock Machine and take over their territory by force. Thus, a representative of Hell's Angels decided to walk into a Rock Machine-owned club and leave a letter.

This may seem like an unusual thing to do, particularly from someone who belongs to one of the most dangerous biker gangs in history, but the contents of the letter showed that Hell's Angels' intentions were far from pure. The letter stated that Rock Machine should no longer consider itself a 1%er club.

This seemingly innocuous statement had an underlying message - that Hell's Angels were planning on taking over territory owned by Rock Machine, and that they were planning on starting an offensive soon.

This naturally set Rock Machine on edge and prompted them to take up arms. Bandidos had also been somewhat unsure of their position within Montreal after Cazzetta got arrested and shared Rock Machine's unease.

But they, too, decided to arm themselves in case Hell's Angels made a move.

This clear indication of aggressive intent ended up doing away with a lot of the progress Boucher had made with his subterfuge-based tactics. Rock Machine recognized the fact that Hell's Angels had set up puppet clubs in order to create discontent among their members.

In many ways, the letter led to the second major event that sparked the war. It was, in fact, the actual starting point of the war. Everything else so far had been preamble events leading to the war that were resulting in rising tensions. The ambition of the leaders of these gangs, the discontent within the gangs themselves, the hunger of the criminal element within Montreal, Cazetta's arrest, the letter, all of these things came together sparking the Quebec Biker War.

Two members of a Hell's Angels puppet club entered a Rock Machine establishment on Boucher's orders to try to convince the manager of the establishment to hand over his illicit investments to Hell's Angels. As it turned out, Bandidos and Rock Machine had put men at every establishment in order to prevent

Hell's Angels puppet clubs from influencing the people managing their locations. When the Hell's Angels puppet club saw members of Bandidos and Rock Machine, they simply opened fire.

In the ensuing shootout, one of the Rock Machine members was killed. Once the shot was fired and the member died, there was no going back. Boucher had not wanted a war, but that did not mean that he was not prepared for one. Bandidos and Rock Machine mounted their troops and began to launch an offensive. Little did they know, Boucher had spent the last decade preparing for war, and he had far more manpower and firepower than both gangs could fight against with their combined forces. The result was blood and destruction for the next eight years.

Once the shots were fired, all-out war erupted. Boucher dipped into his stock of weapons and immediately dispatched requests for resupply to his contacts along with requests for backup to all of his fellow Hell's Angels chapters. Boucher immediately began to threaten street level dealers that if they did not purchase their drugs from Hell's Angels, they would be considered enemies of the organization. He also postulated that anybody who bought any drugs from either Bandidos or Rock Machine would also be considered enemies. Since he had the manpower to support so much aggression, dealers tended to side with him, which caused the Bandidos and Rock Machine's profits to dry up. This put pressure on both organizations and forced them to operate on lower budgets than they were accustomed to.

In order to put further pressure on Bandidos in particular, Boucher approached the Pelletier clan for help. Harold Pelletier, ([20])a notable member of the clan as well as Hell's Angels, had been one of the leaders of the Montreal chapter who had been responsible for the Lennoxville Massacre. Boucher put pressure on the Pelletier clan to help him in this situation, stating that it was Harold Pelletier's brash decision to murder members of his own gang that led to the creation of Rock Machine and arguably was the first event in a series of events that eventually led to the war they were now fighting.

Boucher ordered the Pelletier clan to hire a hit man to target the families of members of Bandidos. He made sure to tell them not to target high-level members but these mid-level members instead. His intention was to scare these mid level members and make them fear for the lives of their families and thus prevent them from becoming too deeply involved in the war. After the girlfriend of a mid-level member of Bandidos was murdered by a Pelletier hit man, Bandidos members began to realize the severity of the situation.

It was a testament to Boucher's intelligence that he did not hire the hit man. Although the targets of his hits knew that the hit man was somehow connected to Boucher and Hell's Angels, police did not have enough evidence to connect him to the actual hits. They traced the killings back to the Pelletier family, and that is where the trail ended. Had he hired the hit man himself, Boucher would have been arrested in no time for assisting in a murder. Him getting taken out so early in the game would have destroyed any chances that Hell's Angels would have had to win the war, as they would have lost their leader at a time when they needed him the most.

Boucher also made sure to show his enemies' intent by not just arming his men with heavy weapons but in engaging in what are nothing less than terrorist activities. These activities involved bombing Rock Machine and Bandidos-owned establishments in order to intimidate them. It must be noted that this was far beyond anything anyone had ever done during a turf war. What Boucher was doing was extreme, even for 1% biker gangs, but in doing so, he told his enemies that there were no rules.

On August 9, 1995, a Jeep exploded in Montreal. The driver, Marc Dubé, was killed instantly. A drug runner, Dubé was just another gang-related death among a string of back-and-forth killings. However, Dubé wasn't the only victim that day. Daniel Desrochers, 11 years old, was riding his bike in the area when the bomb went off and was riddled with shrapnel. Daniel lay in a coma for four days before passing away from his injuries.

The Alliance

It is safe to say that both Bandidos and Rock Machine were utterly shocked by the sheer force with which Hell's Angels hit them. Neither group had any idea that Boucher had been amassing such a stockpile of weapons and that he had acquired so much manpower, so when the war began, they had not been expecting such an assault that would leave them reeling.

All at once their cash flows had begun to dry up, their men had begun to desert them, and they had begun to lose bases in which they could plan counterattacks. They soon realized that they were losing badly, as they had failed to counter even a single one of Hell's Angels attacks by the time they started getting bombed.

Realizing that they were about to lose everything that they had gained after the Lennoxville Massacre, Bandidos decided that instead of being brave, they would be smart. They did not have the manpower to counteract the strength of Hell's Angels, and they were positive that Boucher had called upon his fellow chapters to aid him in his war. He would soon be getting reinforcements from the US if he needed them, and once they began to pour in, there would be nothing left of Bandidos in Canada, not even a memory of their organization.

Therefore, Bandidos approached the Quebec mafia. They owed him, particularly after he had saved Cazzetta from the embarrassment of surrendering his territory to rival gangs. Bandidos had a unique bargaining chip - Boucher had come out in full force far too suddenly. He had brought a great deal of attention to his numbers, and this set great many criminals on edge, including the mafia.

The Quebec mafia agreed to help and started by rooting out Boucher's weapons provider and removing him from the game. This meant that whatever weapons stockpile Boucher had managed to get was all that he would be able to use during the war, and it would be a long while before he would be able to find another weapons provider. This was a crucial move as it helped to balance the scales considerably.

As the Quebec mafia did their part, Bandidos approached the criminal element within Montreal. Everybody knew that Hell's

Angels would be taking over within no time at this rate, and the police had already started to get involved. They had to work together if they didn't want to be subservient to Hell's Angels for the foreseeable future.

Hell's Angels had already strong-armed several dealers into dealing with them and them alone, and the gangs that these dealers belonged to were thoroughly disgruntled. All of these criminal elements came together to form an "Alliance Against Hell's Angels". Heading this alliance, Bandidos and Rock Machine finally had a fighting chance in the war and were able to keep up their defenses for the better part of a decade.

Police and Political Response

All of this death and devastation obviously got the attention of the police as well as politicians. Bikers were always considered nuisances but nothing really to worry about. The Nordic Biker War had been an anomaly, according to the public, and most bikers weren't criminals anyway.

The war showed police and politicians alike the reality of the situation. Immediately law enforcement officials began to approach any sources that could possibly have information to give regarding the criminal elements involved. Police were shocked to find out that practically every criminal element that had a significant presence in Montreal was involved in this war.

As the war progressed, dozens of Hell's Angels and Bandidos members were killed and dozens more arrested. A lot of the times, police didn't even have any charges for the people that were arrested; they just did so to take them off the streets for as long as possible. Despite these arrests, police were unable to make headway until finally they were able to get six members of the Hell's Angels on murder charges. They agreed to let these Hell's Angels members go as long as they became informants and told the police everything that was about to happen before it actually occurred.

This was an important turning point in the war. Once the police were able to place informants within Hell's Angels, they were able to gain intelligence on the major players in the gang. This included Boucher, who soon became the main target. Bandidos members were less easy to turn, but they soon began working with police in order to take Hell's Angels down. The Montreal Police Department, 'Service de police de la Ville de Montréal' (SPVM), saw the virtue of working with the lesser evil, for they saw what Hell's Angels was doing to the city and what they could continue to do if they came into power.

Resolution and Aftermath

The police were eventually able to stop major shootouts before they happened. Boucher became suspicious as a result of this, and he began to suspect many of his closest men of being police informants. Some of his associates thought that he was getting paranoid and was unable to handle the stress of leading this organization during a turf war. Little did they know, Boucher's suspicions, though unfounded, were completely true.

Boucher had one of his men tailed and discovered that he had regularly been meeting with police. In these meetings, the man had been disclosing extremely sensitive information to these law enforcement officials, information that had led to the beginning of a slow decline in his campaign against Bandidos and Rock Machine. Boucher had this member of his gang killed.

It is a testament to what a cool and clear-headed mind Boucher had that he did not go into panic mode. Rather than starting to doubt every single one of his men, he decided to take the fight to the police.

Boucher kidnapped two correctional officers who had been involved in making deals with some of his men who was an associate of his by the name of Stephane Gagne. He killed both of these correctional officers in order to discourage the police from attempting to turn his bikers into informants.

This turned out to be extremely effective. Over the next few years, his Hell's Angels began to get the upper hand in the war. The smaller gangs decided to run rather than be decimated, the mafia were able to become suppliers in their own rights once more and thus had no need to be involved in the war, preferring to manage and protect their own assets. And in the end, Bandidos and Rock Machine were left to fight the war on their own.

Six years after the war began, Rock Machine's numbers were too low for it to continue to call itself a motorcycle club. Thus, Bandidos decided to offer patched memberships to all Rock Machine members in order to bolster their own numbers. Hell's Angels had also suffered great losses but firmly held the upper hand.

However, Boucher's killing of the correctional officers, effective though it was, turned out to be his undoing when Gagne was arrested by the police and charged with murder. He agreed to testify against Boucher in exchange for receiving a reduced sentence. Boucher was convicted of two counts of first-degree murder in 2002 and sentenced to 25 years in prison.

Hell's Angels successfully managed to secure their interests in Montreal. After the war, they became equal to the Quebec mafia in terms of the drug trade, as Boucher had left good men behind who knew how to take care of the organization. The losses Bandidos suffered during the war were so great that they were forced to close their doors permanently approximately four years after the war. Rock Machine was re-established as a strictly crime-free motorcycle club shortly thereafter.

Major Players in the War

There were several individuals without whom the war would either not have started or would not have been nearly as bloody. These people were essential to the genesis of the conflict that led to the war, or they were responsible for the events that would lead to the war ending finally in 2002. It is important to study these people and to examine their personalities. Understanding the people that cause such destruction can allow us to prevent such things from happening in the future

1) Maurice Boucher

Perhaps the single most important member of the Hell's Angels during the war, Boucher is the man that started the war and it was his eventual conviction that lead to its end. His leadership was an important part of what made Hell's Angels in Canada strong enough to fight the war for so long, but it should also be noted that he was not just a thug. Boucher was, in fact, a shrewd leader, one that favored strategy and subterfuge over all-out war. It was his leadership that led to the war being dragged out for so long.

An interesting thing to note is that Boucher was reported to be racist by Canadian media. But this portrayal of him was a fabrication ostensibly created in order to turn the public against him and make him as villainous a figure as possible. Far from being racist, Boucher's best friend and protector was black, a man by the name of Gregory Wooley. Although him not being racist does not make him any less despicable and responsible for the lives lost during the war, it is interesting to note how the media portrays certain people in order to mold public perception.

2) Stephane Gagne

Gagne is important in relation to Boucher because of his aforementioned role in ending the war. He was an important part of the Hell's Angels organization, and it was this elevated status that led him to being such a key part of the eventual prosecution against Boucher. It is important to note that Gagne was extremely faithful to the Hell's Angels cause. It was only when he was faced with prosecution that he decided that it would be better to bear witness against the leading members of Hell's Angels and get a reduced sentence rather than face a full quarter-century in a maximum security prison.

3) Patrick Call

Patrick Call is an essential part of this list because it was his actions, or his bullets rather, that ended up sparking the actual war. Call was a Prospect with Hell's Angels when Cazzetta was arrested, and he was one of the first people approached by Boucher and asked to prove himself. Call had always been eager to receive the honor of becoming a patched member of Hell's Angels, and in Boucher's request, he saw an opportunity to finally prove himself worthy of his patch.

As you have probably guessed based on the information provided in previous sections of this chapter, Call was approached by Boucher and asked to form a puppet group that would go around to Rock Machine-owned establishments and put the idea into the owners' heads to sell off their illegal assets to Hell's Angels and join their organization instead. Call was never very good at making offers without intimidating, despite Boucher's frequent requests to tone down the aggression and try to make the targets feel as though he was on their side.

Eventually, Call's aggression got the best of him. Inspired by the subtly threatening letter his associates had dropped off at a Rock Machine club, Call decided to open fire when he saw members of Bandidos and Rock Machine at an establishment he was supposed to negotiate with. He killed a member of Rock Machine, thereby properly starting the war.

4) Harold Pelletier, Luc Michaud, Rejean Lessard and Robert Tremblay

These four individuals hold extraordinary importance, not in the war itself, but in the events leading up to the war. Pelletier, Michaud, Lessard and Tremblay were the leaders of the Quebec-based chapters of Hell's Angels. It was they who were responsible for overseeing the manufacturing of meth within their chapters and to ship this meth to fellow Hell's Angels chapters in the north.

They were given the short shrift by these Hell's Angels chapters that were skimming from the profits and consuming all of the drugs that they were supposed to sell. It was these four individuals that invited members from these northern chapters to a party where they shot them down in an event that would come to be known as the Lennoxville Massacre.

It can be said that it was Pelletier, Michaud, Lessad and Tremblay who sparked the series of events that would culminate in the Quebec Biker War.

5) Salvatore Cazzetta

Cazzetta and Boucher are appropriate bookends to this list as it was their cold war that led to the Quebec Biker War, although Cazzetta was not involved in the war, being in prison at the time. Cazzetta's ambition and his drive was what led to Rock Machine becoming its own entity, Rock Machine collaborating with Bandidos, and his acquisition of a regular consignment of drugs, each of which was instrumental in fanning the flames of inter-gang tensions, as well as his eventual downfall. Both of the aforementioned results of his activities were crucial to the eventual war.

Cazzetta was different from Boucher in that he had a much more focused approach to his crime. He wanted to be the man in charge and he wanted to do it on his own. Where Boucher was not afraid to humble himself in front of powerful people, even within his own gang, in order to prepare for war, Cazzetta bowed to no one, instead wanting people to pay him tribute and to come to him for his services. This ideology was shaped mostly by his upbringing in a mafia family, where he was always expected to make something of himself.

***

All in all, the thing that really led to the war was when the fine line was crossed between ambition and greed. Even criminals have a code, a code that ensures that minimal losses occur. The Quebec Biker War broke every aspect of that code. It can be argued that this war ended up shaping the near future, the time that we refer to as the present. With Rock Machine absorbed into Bandidos and Hell's Angels a reckoning force, the most important thing to note is that the police are now involved and are more aware of the dangers that these groups, the 1%ers, pose.

About Crimes Canada: True Crimes That Shocked the Nation

This is a multi-volume twenty-four book collection, (one per month, each approximately 100 to 180 pages) project by crime historian Dr. Peter Vronsky and true crime author and publisher RJ Parker, depicting some of Canada's most notorious criminals.

Crimes Canada: True Crimes that Shocked the Nation will feature a series of Canadian true crime short-read books published by *VP Publications* (Vronsky & Parker), an imprint of *RJ Parker Publishing, Inc.*, one of North America's leading publishers of true crime.

Peter Vronsky is the bestselling author of *Serial Killers: The Method and Madness of Monsters* and *Female Serial Killers: How and Why Women Become Monsters* while RJ Parker is not only a successful publisher but also the author of 18 books, including *Serial Killers Abridged: An Encyclopedia of 100 Serial Killers*, *Parents Who Killed Their Children: Filicide*, and *Serial Killer Groupies*. Both are Canadians and have teamed up to share shocking Canadian true crime cases not only with fellow Canadian readers but with Americans and world readers as well, who will be shocked and horrified by just how evil and sick "nice" Canadians can be when they go bad.

Finally, we invite fellow Canadians, aspiring or established authors, to submit proposals or manuscripts to *VP Publications* at *Editors@CrimesCanada.com*.

VP Publications is a new frontier traditional publisher, offering their published authors a generous royalty agreement payable within three months of publishing and aggressive online marketing support. Unlike many so-called "publishers" that are nothing but vanity presses in disguise, VP Publications does not charge authors in advance for submitting their proposal or manuscripts, nor do we charge authors if we choose to publish their works. We pay you, and pay well.

Thank you to my editor, proof-readers, and cover artist for your support:

- - RJ

Aeternum Designs (book cover)
Bettye McKee (editor)
Dr. Peter Vronsky (editor)
Lorrie Suzanne Phillippe
Marlene Fabregas
Darlene Horn
Ron Steed
June Julie Dechman
Katherine McCarthy
Robyn MacEachern
Mary Daniels
Kim Jackson
Paul Bradbury

An exciting 24-volume series collection, edited by crime historian Dr. Peter Vronsky and true crime author and publisher RJ Parker.

Robert Pickton: The Pig Farmer Killer (Volume 1)
By Chris Swinney

Robert Pickton inherited a pig farm worth a million dollars and used his wealth to lure skid row hookers to his farm where he confessed to murdering 49 female victims; dismembering and feeding their body parts to his pigs, which he supplied to Vancouver area restaurants and local neighbors.

Marc Lépine: The Montreal Massacre (Volume 2)
By RJ Parker

With extreme hatred in his heart against feminism, an act that feminists would label 'gynocide,' a heavily armed Marc Lépine entered the University École Polytechnique de Montreal, and after allowing the male students to leave, systematically murdered 14 female students.

But what motivated Lépine to carry out this heinous crime? Mass murderer, madman, cold-blooded killer, misogynist, political zealot? Or was he simply another desperate person frustrated with his powerless status in this world?

Only one thing is known for sure - Lépine's actions on December 6, 1989 radically changed this country and why he did what he did is much more complex than we will ever know.

Paul Bernardo and Karla Homolka: The Ken and Barbie Killers (Volume 3)
By Peter Vronsky

Paul Bernardo and Karla Homolka were so perfectly iconic as a newlywed couple that they were dubbed "Ken and Barbie". But their marriage had a dark side involving sex, death, and videotape. The 'perfect couple' first raped and murdered Karla's little sister and then kidnapped teenage schoolgirls whom they enslaved, raped, tortured and killed while gleefully recording themselves on video doing it. Vronsky will take you on the journey from the Scarborough Rapist (Bernardo) to Bordelais (Homolka's current last name) and her return to Canada in October 2014 from the island of Gaudeloupe, where she lived for several years with her husband and three children.

Shirley Turner: Doctor, Stalker, Murderer (Volume 4)

By Kelly Banaski

On November 6, 2001, Dr. Andrew Bagby was found dead in a parking lot for day use at Keystone State Park in Derry Township, Pennsylvania. He had been shot to death. There were five gunshot wounds as well as blunt force trauma to the back of the head. He had been shot in the face and chest, as well as the back of the head, back, and buttocks. He was left face down in the parking lot in his scrubs, next to his Toyota Corolla. He died there.

The bizarre murder case of Andrew Bagby entails far more than death, although it has that threefold. It also brought to light a woefully inept Canadian legal system and the frighteningly dark mental descent of a woman scorned.

While evidence was steadily mounting against her, Dr. Shirley Turner dropped everything, left her car, apartment and every worldly possession, and went back to Canada. By the time

Pennsylvania had an open warrant on her, she was in St. John's, Newfoundland, Canada. There, she gave birth to Andrew's son, Zachary.

While in jail, she wrote to a judge. Against legal precedent, this judge wrote her back and gave her legal advice on how to proceed with her case. The United States presented evidence of her crimes and their investigation and findings thus far. It was overwhelming. Her lies were exposed, her gun casings matched, and witnesses placed her car next to his at the time of the murder.

What happened next is one of the strangest decisions in legal history.

Canadian Psycho: The True Story of Luka Magnotta (Volume 5)
By Cara Lee Carter

Murder, necrophilia, dismemberment and an international manhunt – while the case of Luka Magnotta reads like a work of fiction, it is in fact a true story of an individual with a long history of mental illness in a gruesome attempt to gain notoriety. The horrific murder and mutilation of 32-year-old Concordia student Lin Jun shocked and captivated the nation. From the time the body was discovered, to the capture of Magnotta, and through the ensuing two years it took for justice to be served, the country anxiously waited for the outcome of the trial in December of 2014. This book chronicles the journey that led Luka Magnotta to become known as the Canadian Psycho. **WITH PHOTOS** (Warning: Crime scene photos included that some might find extremely disturbing).

The Country Boy Killer: The True Story of Cody Legebokoff, Canada's Teenage Serial Killer (Volume 6)
By JT Hunter

He was the friendly, baby-faced, Canadian boy next door. He came from a loving, caring, and well-respected family. Blessed with good looks and back-woods country charm, he was popular with his peers, and although an accident at birth left permanent nerve damage in one of his arms, he excelled in sports. A self-proclaimed "die hard" Calgary Flames fan, he played competitive junior hockey and competed on his school's snowboarding team. And he enjoyed the typical simple pleasures of a boy growing up in the country: camping, hunting, and fishing with family and friends. But he also enjoyed brutally murdering women, and he would become one of the youngest serial killers in Canadian history.

The Killer Handyman (Volume 7)

By C.L. Swinney

A harmless-looking man moved to Montreal looking for a new start and to get off drugs. Somewhere along the line, his urge to prey on unsuspecting women, something he'd done and kept a secret for twenty years, became too much to keep inside. William Fyfe, aka "The Killer Handyman," snapped, leaving at least nine women brutally beaten, murdered and sexual abused (post-mortem). If not for the diligent work of a criminal forensic specialist and her discovery of a single fingerprint, Fyfe may have continued to kill at will, keeping Montreal residents, particularly single middle-aged women, frightened and sequestered in their own homes.

Hell's Angels Biker Wars: The Rock Machine Massacres (Volume 8)

By RJ Parker

For eight years, two outlaw biker clubs fought to control street-level drug sales in Quebec, Canada. The notorious Hells Angels went up against local drug dealers, the Mafia, and a rival biker club, the Rock Machine. Bombings and bullets was no stranger in the streets and many unfortunate bystanders got caught in the crossfire. When the smoke cleared and dozens of outlaws arrested, over 150 people were dead.

This true crime book depicts the history of both clubs and the events known as the Quebec Biker War.

Other True Crime Books by
RJ Parker Publishing

Forensic Analysis and DNA in Criminal Investigations: Including Cold Cases Solved.

By RJ Parker

Released October 7, 2015

Including several cold cases that were most recently solved using forensic analysis. Also, the pros and cons of forensic science.

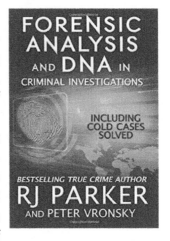

From ballistics and blood splatter patterns to DNA analysis and voice printing, RJ Parker explores the highly complex world of investigative forensic sciences. Intended as an introductory guide and reference to forensic techniques for front-line police officers, criminal attorneys, journalists, crime authors and just interested readers, this encyclopedic book is a must read for any true crime aficionado.

Parker examines various forensic techniques and principles of investigative sciences, some of the historical figures in the evolution of forensics over the last two centuries, and provides real cold case examples where forensic sciences were key to not only in identifying the guilty but also in clearing the innocent and freeing the wrongly convicted.

Till Death Do Us Part: A Collection of Newlywed Murder Cases

By JJ Slate

Released February 28, 2015

Studies have shown that marriages typically thrive the most in the months after the wedding, a period known as "the honeymoon period."

Not these marriages.

Spousal murder is never acceptable, but newlywed murder seems to be on a completely different level. It is unconscionable to think someone could stand in front of his family and friends, pledging to honor and cherish another person for the rest of his life, and then kill his spouse in cold blood just months, weeks, or even days later. It happens more than you'd think—and, contrary to popular belief, it's not always the husband who acts as the aggressor.

In her third true crime book, bestselling author JJ Slate examines more than twenty true stories of newlywed murders, delving into the past of the victims and aggressors, searching for answers to the question everyone is asking: How does this sort of thing happen? These shocking cases of betrayal and murder might just make you think differently about those five sacred words, "till death do us part."

Serial Killer Groupies

By RJ Parker

Released January 1, 2015

This book delves into the twisted psychology of women attracted to some of the most notorious monsters on the planet, giving true crime readers real insight into this phenomenon.

One of the most common reasons given by women who date serial killers is the fact that they 'see' the little boy that the horrible man once used to be, and they believe that they can nurture that kid, hence removing the cruel and harmful nature of the killers and making them amicable again.

Known as 'serial killer groupies' or even 'prison groupies' by some, a great number of these women have shown a surprising desire to get connected to the serial killer of their choice. Many of these women have become directly aligned with these killers, and some have even married these hardened criminals.

Groupies will do almost anything to get close to the prisoner they are attracted to. They give up jobs, family, spend money on him, and even move across country to be in the same town as him.

Some SKGs are attracted to the celebrity status they acquire. They go on talk shows to announce their undying love for the serial killer and proclaim that he was not capable of these killings.

Missing Wives, Missing Lives

By JJ Slate

Released June 16, 2014

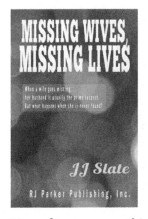

When a wife goes missing, her husband is often the prime suspect in her disappearance. But what happens when she is never found? In some of the cases profiled in this chilling book, their husbands were found guilty of murder, even without a body.

Missing Wives, Missing Lives focuses on thirty unique cases in which a missing wife has never been found and the undying efforts of her family as they continue the painful search to bring her home. The book covers decades old cases, such as Jeanette Zapata, who has been missing since 1976, to more recent and widely known cases, such as Stacy Peterson, who has been missing since 2007. Keeping these women's stories alive may be the key to solving the mystery and bringing them home to their family.

Social Media Monsters: Internet Killers

By JJ Slate and RJ Parker

Released September 18, 2014

In July of 2009, twenty-one-year-old Heather Snively logged onto Craigslist in search of used baby clothes and toys. She was eight months pregnant with her first child and so excited to marry her fiancé and start their family. She never imagined the woman she contacted on the site had 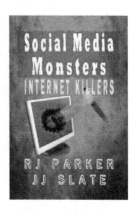 plans to murder her in cold blood and rip the baby from her womb.

Who is really on the other end of that Facebook friend request, or behind that dating profile, or posting that item for sale on Craigslist? How can you be safe if you plan to meet up with a stranger you met online? What precautions should you take?

In this book, we've detailed more than thirty chilling true stories of killers that have used the internet to locate, stalk, lure, or exploit their victims. Facebook, Craigslist, MySpace, chat rooms, dating sites—it does not matter where you are online; killers are lurking in the shadows. They visit suicide chat rooms, search for escorts on Craigslist, and create fake social media profiles to fool and gain the trust of their victims. Someone you have been talking to for months, or even years, could be a completely different person from what you envisioned.

Serial Killers Abridged: An Encyclopedia of 100 Serial Killers

By RJ Parker

Released May 31, 2014

WARNING: There are dramatic crime scene photos in this book that some may find very disturbing

The ultimate reference for anyone compelled by the pathologies and twisted minds behind the most disturbing homicidal monsters. From A to Z, there are names you may not have heard of, but many of you are familiar with, including the notorious John Wayne Gacy, Jeffrey Dahmer, Ted Bundy, Gary Ridgway, Aileen Wuornos, and Dennis Rader, just to name a few. This reference book will make a great collection for true crime enthusiasts. Each story is in a Reader's Digest short format.

Parents Who Killed their Children: Filicide

By RJ Parker

Released April 30, 2014

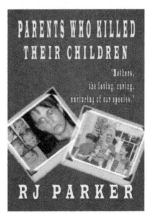

What could possibly incite parents to kill their own children?

This collection of "Filicidal Killers" provides a gripping overview of how things can go horribly wrong in once-loving families. *Parents Who Killed their Children* depicts ten of the most notorious and horrific cases of homicidal parental units out of control. Included are the stories of Andrea Yates, Diane Downs, Susan Smith, and Jeffrey MacDonald, who received a great deal of media attention. The author explores the reasons behind these murders; from addiction to postpartum psychosis, insanity to altruism.

Each story is detailed with background information on the parents, the murder scenes, trials, sentencing and aftermath.

About the Author

RJ Parker, P.Mgr., MCrim, is an award-winning and bestselling true crime author and publisher of RJ Parker Publishing. He has written 18 true crime books including "_Forensic Analysis and DNA in Criminal Investigations: Including Cold Cases Solved_," which was released on October 4, 2015. He holds Certifications in Serial Crime and Criminal Profiling.

"Parker amazes his readers with top notch writing and idealist research. The Canadian writer has a better grasp of criminology and the psyche of a serial killer's mind than most people who spend a lifetime in a professional field chasing criminals and diabolic fiends."

— **John Douglas** (Ret'd FBI Agent), Author of *MINDHUNTERS*

Besides gifting books to his cause, Wounded Warriors, and donating to Victims of Violent Crimes, RJ has daily contests on Facebook where he gifts eBooks and autographed books.

RJ Parker was born and raised in Newfoundland and now resides in Ontario and Newfoundland, Canada. He spent twenty-five years in various facets of Government and has two professional designations. In his spare time, RJ enjoys playing the guitar, mandolin, piano, drums, steel guitar and sax.

** SIGN UP FOR OUR MONTLY NEWSLETTER *http://rjpp.ca/RJ-PARKER-NEWSLETTER* **

CONTACT INFORMATION

Facebook
http://www.facebook.com/RJParkerPublishing
Email - AuthorRJParker@Gmail.Com
Email - Agent@RJParkerPublishing.com
Website - www.RJParkerPublishing.com
Twitter - @AuthorRJParker

1   http://hbmm-national.org/how-hbmm-operates/a-little-biker-education/understanding-the-biker-culture

2   http://www.corrections.com/news/article/25849-biker-gangs-have-deep-roots

3   http://www.azlyrics.com/lyrics/steppenwolf/borntobewild.html

4   http://www.meth-kills.org/history-of-meth.html

5   http://www.citynews.ca/2007/04/04/overview-of-biker-gangs-history-in-canada/

6   http://www.outlawsmcworld.com/onepercenter.htm

7   https://stylewallbybecca.files.wordpress.com/2012/02/uniform-freedom-in-biker-dress-embodying-identity-through-subcultural-style-docx-3.pdf

8   http://www.adl.org/combating-hate/domestic-extremism-terrorism/c/bigots-on-bikes.html?referrer=https://www.google.ca/#.VgLUSa5Viko

9   http://affa.hells-angels.com/hamc-history/

10 http://www.pobobmc.com/history.html

11 http://auto.howstuffworks.com/hells-angels2.htm

12 http://bandidosranders.dk/bmc/index.php?option=com_content&view=article&id=3&Itemid=2

13 http://heavy.com/news/2015/05/bandidos-motorcycle-club-biker-gang-waco-texas-shooting-shootout-rivals-scimitars-cossacks-photos-founded-motto-patch/

14 https://prezi.com/4dvpfwfwcrz-/the-bandidos/

15 http://outlawbikergangs.blogspot.ca/

16 https://en.wikipedia.org/wiki/Lennoxville_massacre

17 http://murderpedia.org/male.B/b/boucher-maurice.htm

18 http://www.oocities.org/wiseguywally/SalvatoreCazzetta.html

19 http://murderpedia.org/male.B/b/boucher-maurice.htm

20 http://www.oocities.org/wiseguywally/HaroldPelletier.html

Made in the USA
Las Vegas, NV
25 April 2023